Byrdie's Songs:

A Collection of Poetry

by Kenya Wilcox

RoseDog Books
PITTSBURGH, PENNSYLVANIA 15238

RoseDog Books
585 Alpha Drive
Suite 103
Pittsburgh, PA 15238
Visit our website at *www.rosedogbookstore.com*

ISBN: 979-8-88527-915-4
eISBN: 979-8-88527-963-5

Byrdie's Songs:

A Collection of Poetry

I DREAMED OF YOU

I dreamed of you
Before there was a name
I would have visions of your smile
And eyes that make the finest explorer get lost in

It's mesmerizing how the sun hits your skin
Light brown hue showing the complexity of your eyelashes
Highlighting the tip of your button nose
While showing the sandy brown in the edges of your hair

So adorable, how you raise your hands when your favorite song comes on
I am compelled to cover your face with kisses of admiration
Never to let you out of my sight
Even if it's to watch you sleep in my arms

I never knew love until God trusted me enough to have you
The way I get lost in the dimples in your cheeks
Makes me thank God for your innocence
And your zeal for life

Oh God, how I love you
Your presence speaks volume to my soul
With each laughter, pout, and tantrum
There is beauty in all that you are

And now that you are my reality
I can't help but try to freeze time
To when I very first met you
In my dream

Mommy loves you, Ian

WE'VE COME TOO FAR

Verse: You say that we would be together

Not just today but until forever
We've been having ups and downs
But we can still work it out
Reminiscing on how it used to be
Dreams of having a family
Your love for me drifted away
Oh baby, why didn't you stay

Chorus: I ain't got no words to say

Because he packed his bags and he left today. Oh baby, how could this be. Because we've come too far for you to leave me.
Yeah

Verse: All I can do is think about you

I thought you would always be my boo
Now what am I supposed to do?
I wish this nightmare wasn't true
Now he's gone and I don't know why
He didn't even say goodbye
I woke up to a four-page letter
Saying that we can't continue to be together

Chorus (2x)

Bridge: O why, oh why, oh why

Did you have to say goodbye (oh why, oh why)
You were apple of my eye (oh why, oh why)

And since you're gone baby all I can do cry

Chorus

Oh, come back baby, come back home
I can't stand being alone
Oh baby, please
I come too far for you to leave me, baby
Oh baby, no not right now
I need you, oh baby
I say we've come too far for you to leave me

   End

BABE RUTH

Excuse me for my words
I'm trying to make myself clear
When I think about it, I shed a tear
'Cuz I been chasing you for about a year

And as my heartbeat grows fast
Every minute you passed
I want to put you in slow motion
So, your footsteps will last

Baby you are the planets
Let me surround you like a moon
Touching every part of your atmosphere
Meteor showers bloom

Like a flower
You are my April showers
Being with you is not just a pleasure
But a fire and desire

Oh, so fine and dandy
My chocolate candy
I get so mesmerized by those caramel eyes
That got me so hypnotized

I just wanna
Get chocolate wasted in between your thighs
Drown me with your milky way
In the middle holds sweet juice

You are my Babe Ruth
Holding nothing but the truth

I swear baby
My twisted nerves got me

Stumbling over my words
'Cuz when I see your face
Bullshit is for the birds
Because you're nothing but the truth

I told you before, you're like a Babe Ruth
The way you walk and the way you talk
Got my curiosity at a boost
Baby I want you near me
To hold me and possibly love me
I was blinded by your love
and I'm seeing clearly that
You are my Babe Ruth

Holding nothing
NOTHING
but the truth

GIVE INTO ME

I want you
I mean not just to touch my insides
I want you to, poetically
Get lost in between my thighs

Make love to me
Not just with your touch
But allow your eyes to dance
Up and down with every thrust

Give into me
Every inch of your anatomy
The grunts and whispers in my ear
There's no place I rather be

Tell me how you want it
For you I make myself available
In the bed, on a chair, tied up
I'll be flexible

You unleashed the very freak in me
When you reached the bottom of my wetness
I swear I love when you choke me with every stroke
You handle my flower so reckless

So, pluck my flower
Drink every drop of my nectar
As we come for each other
Over and over

BACK TO THE PRONOUNS

There was a time when
I loved being with her but a higher being tells me to be with him
I swear it felt so right when it's wrong with her but man I...
I got to be right or close to right
Or I'll be in a place that's wrong
There was a time when
Kissing her was better than
Kissing him and slowly I became
Them and in them I drifted away
From Him...going, going gone
Or was I?

I know they will bring up my past
You're too late I'll do it myself
Rewind and let me tell it, I know how it went

There was a time when
Yeah, I kissed her, sweet as honey
Me and her became we and I planned
Us
But the more I thought I loved her
And the more she lusted me I felt like
A sting of death inside of me
She song in grace and harmony, but the more the song played the more
my side got numb from her sting
The more she "loved" me, the sting got powerful and my grave was
calling my name loud as hell
But enough about the old me

I got tired of the sting
When I lost sight of Him when

I became them so I had to
Separate from them to be
Close to Him so I can get back
To me and I feel well almost free

My mind still plays tricks on me
Yeah, I occasionally think about she
And what we would be
But He is still working on me so I
Lose sight of she so I won't lose me again

The more I talked to Him
The more I knew me
I see clearly that He is in me
And without Him there is no me
So, what am I?
Invisible...going, going gone
Or am I?

I swear when I talk to Him
I am happy, because I'm me
It's me but I ask Him can I
Go back to them not to lead
Or join but enlighten them
Don't keep getting lost in them
Because it separates you from
Him and without him you are
Nonexistent....going, going gone
Or are you?

There will be a time when
All knees will bow to Him
That loves us
I'm not all the way right with Him
But I'm trying and them can do it, too

Being with Him
Got me back to me
And them has hope to get back to you
And we can dwell with Him forever
Up, up, and away

Back to Me
Back to you
Back to us
Back with Him

GIVE ME LIFE

Saying -"I love you" is like having a heart attack and passing away, but them telling you they love you back is like a defibrillator to the heart that brings you back to life. Baby, I'm waiting for you to revive me.

Mouth to mouth resuscitation
Your truth running through my veins
Your kiss is my blood circulation
The way I breathe ain't the same

Keep breathing love into me
Your love inside of me
Reaching every organ
I can fully see

I'm almost here
Just give me breath once more
In my tunnel of darkness
You are my door

From my eyes you seem blurry
Gripping my hand, trying to believe
"I love you too, baby"
I got a pulse, IM BREATHING!

GOLDIGGING HEIFER

Verse:

Walking around with all your bling
Do you have me some spending money
For me to blow
Your wallet empty
I don't date cheap
I need some new shoes for my feet
My middle name is free

Ooh your mouth is saying let's go
But your wallet saying hell no

Chorus:

If you wanna be with me
You got to buy me some jewelry
I'm a goldigging heifer
You gotta buy my love from me (2x)
Imma goldigging heifer baby
Gotta buy my love from me yeah (2x)

Verse:

So, get out my face, boy
You wasting my time
You broke as hell
You ain't got a dime
I ain't with that
So, find me someone with some cash
And my love for him is gonna last
Until he runs out (aw well)

Ooh your mouth is saying let's go
But your wallet saying hell no

Chorus

Imma golddigging heifer (2x)
Imma golddigging heifer, baby
Give, give, give me all your money

End

IF I COULD

If only I could
Rewind the hands of time
I would press play on
The times you were still mines

If I could pause the moment
With a blink of an eye
I would hug and kiss you
While we sat side by side

If I could stop that day
That you left to be with Thee
I would cradle you in my arms, my child
Until you felt content and free

But I press forward and began to see
That you left without hesitation
To serve and rest with God
Who orchestrates a Holy nation

I miss you my child
I will feel your presence forever
I can't wait until I see you again
So, we can praise and serve God together

I'M JUST...

The Lord is my Shepherd
And I am their pastor
Lord, you told me that this duty will have its
Triumphs and disasters

Thirty years in this building
This journey I dare not regret
My heart is still beating and I'm still moving
The Lord ain't done with me yet

As I walk with you side by side
Using your Love as a guide
Even the people I pray for get jealous
For in my heart, You reside

Oh God I'm just a servant
Sowing goods seeds in your field
By Your stripes I am healed
By faith, You're my shield

Though the harvest is plentiful
And the laborers are few
At times I discourage at my position
But there's still work to do

I am grateful for being Your Child
The task you assigned me, hmph I can't complain
As I walk in this building, and persecution
I stand by my God in this place unashamed

Oh God, I am just a messenger
Telling them exactly what you told me
Through Your Word I know they're free

Those You've made free, indeed

Telling people about you gave me knowledge
But in You, there's a wiser fear
Obedient lips do solemnly pledge
To speak truth-no tickling ears

Oh God, I'm just a pastor
Grateful to be in Your plan
When I want to throw in the towel
You still hold my hand

Though many people planned for me the worst
You gave me the very best
This life I live on earth
Is only a test

I am designed to give you more
My resolve is never less
So, when I see you in heaven
I'll have an abundant rest

Oh God, I'm not just a Pastor
I am much more than they see
A Father, a friend, a messenger, a servant
And so may things You've blessed me to be

As you look at my journey
I hope that you understand
My God ordained my purpose
And in His Will, ever I stand

I am a Pastor
My testimony is visible to all who can see
That God can shine though you
Because I know that he shines through me

LOVER AND FRIEND

Oh, the annoying assurance
The battle I have within
At war with the heart of my lover
And the spirit of my friend

My friend has known me forever
My lover for only a spell
My lover is only seen in my latest development
But my friend was there before the emergence from my shell

The battle is intense
I want relief
In the prince of my desires
Or the compassion of my commander and chief

Both of them fight for my love
They eternally achieve
but Friend tugs at my heart and Lover is at my sleeve

My friend does not force me
My lover is a persuasion
Is it a gateway of happiness?
Or a fortress of temptation

If I had to choose
I would choose my friend
For He has been there through it all
And is my peace within

ODE TO MR.

Hello, Mr.
How are you?
I've been lied to for so long
That I don't know that if you are the truth

You see I wanted lifetimes
But I ended up with seasons
Visions of you kissing me Mr.
It gives me reasons
To trust you

The talks we have are innocent
Sometimes I think you, heaven sent
Is this a man or just a boy?
Giving me happiness or false joy

Oh Mr. why do you tease me?
I think I like you very much indeed
Sometimes I see that you want to love me
But is my mind playing tricks on me?
Again

I've been hurt by so many
Broken and shattered
Living in pain
My broken pieces I gathered
Alone

No other heart to call my home
So, I would roam
Into others' lives hoping to find
A love of my life

But that is not my job to do
Mr., I see that is your qualification
To see me and establish a nation
Under Him

Are you my liberty or my death?
My knight or the weakening of my emotional health
Give me kisses to make my heart quiver
Or break my trust, leaving me crying like a river

Mr. tell me who you are
You are damn near perfect by far
But I can't get my hopes up
Because love can't be puffed up

You may be a lie
But how do I know
Unless you tell me why you are here
The feelings you have you endlessly show

Persistent you are to me
Why do you try to love me?
Whom you seek
Is this real or am I dreaming?

If I am don't wake me up
I'm tired of drinking heartbreaks bitter cup
Mr tell me again who you are
You are damn near perfect by far

I swear this ain't real
When you talk to me, I blush with flirty chills
Honeybee you call me, because to you I'm sweet
but if you hurt me, you might feel my heart's sting

Mr., tell me who you are
You are damn near perfect by far

And you tell me
"Why miss lady, I am nothing more
than a fighter for your affection"
"It is my obsession to have you as my possession"
"I want to teach you a lesson"
"That if you let me then I can be a blessing"
"To you"

If I let you...

PLASTIC

Look at me, I am perfect indeed
Or are your eyes deceived
I wasn't fortunate to be crafted by the Almighty
But was designed highly by a puffed-up version of society
My blonde hair, blue eyes, thin lips
Small waist, sculpted ass, and nice hips
Hollywood blows up my head when I'm only a fragment of what beauty should be
I am the core of every girl's insecurity
I am plastic
I am the Barbie of your generation
Designed to distort the nation and
Shake every girl's foundation
I am plastic
Little girls now model themselves after me
Because they think that I am true beauty, but their beauty is far more beautiful
than I could ever be because I am
Plastic
I have no feelings, no aspiration, no goals or self-worth
I don't have that special gift each girl has at birth
Since beauty is in the eye of the beholder, that makes you beautiful by default
Unlike me, you are precious and priceless but for a price I am bought
I was bought and brought here to play with your minds like a doll with its owner
Prostituting each girl's self-esteem so Hollywood can get its boner
I am plastic and finally, I'm tired of being fake
I am tired of you trying to look like me when I despise what I was brought
here to be
Little girl you are more than what Hollywood tries to throw on you.
I speak to you now because what I say is true
I give you permission to melt away all of my plastic
And in the melting, I hope you see yourself, the beautiful and wonderful girl
that you were destined to be
And most importantly NOT PLASTIC

REPENTING ADULTERER

I am an adulterer
And when I say this, I shed tears
Because while I was with Him
I was chasing others for over a year

And every night that I slept
The seduction it crept
In between my legs I felt
Ecstasy

I cheated on Him with many hers
It wasn't just the ones with apple
Bottom jeans and boots with fur
But one that look like Him and one who look like both

Oh, I loved them all
You see
Loving her was beautiful
Kissing her was musical
But trying to fuck her was not mutual

Any man would go off on me
If I cheat but you would see me and
Whisper I love you so why do this to me
Your voice would haunt me the more I
Creep

I used to toss and turn while I sleep
Because my feelings for her were so deep
Why did I turn this affair into a celebrity?

I lost sight of my man
I lost sight of what we shared
Even though I hurt him
He still had a heart to care

Even when I wanted to be with her
He still was trying to fulfill my needs
What kind of bitch am I to be?
To cheat on him that loves me
In spite of

I swear he would speak to me
While I was with her
Telling me don't get so mesmerized
By those caramel eyes they blind you
Don't get chocolate wasted in her thighs
The poison is true
Don't call her your Babe Ruth because the feelings y'all share are nothing but a lie and not the truth

Sometimes I cry
Because I lost sight of my guy
That's been there for me
Through it all

In the midst of my fall
He heard my call
He's Telling me to come to him
she is just a fallacy, a poisonous
Ball of ecstasy
You and her can never be because she ain't where you really want to be
And that's with me

Reality check!

Baby, I'm sorry
I already have been forgiven
He forgot about it the very -moment
I said it, I felt it-, it's done

When I went back to him
He made me fall back in love with
His poetry
Like "Oh taste and see that I am good and my mercy endured forever"
Oh, my man is so clever

By himself he weathered
All the storms of my life
All my troubles I put on him
My worries are out of site

His yoke is easy and his burden
Is light
His poetry lets me know that I don't have to fight

In the midst of him fighting
He lets me know that
He wants me
Oh yes, -me
And imma give me back to him
I'm forgiven

THE LIGHT WITHIN THE GRAVE

Oh, what an aching departure
My heart begins to feel
A pain that no song or words of kindness
Could ever heal

My heart is in distress
My anger stares at your grave
I ask God what is the occasion
To not let death behave

The person who warmed me with joy
As they held my hand
Now let's go without hesitation
And walks to the promise land

As the choir sings a song of cheer
My heart is deaf with ears
Although it is a celebration of new life
My soul aches with worldly tears

As your resting place is sealed
I see God shining through
Your peace is well established
The glory of Thee lives in you

I bid you goodbye
For I'll see you soon
In a place of the highest Majesty
Where flowers forever bloom

No sickness shall hinder you
Your life has just begun

Every battle your flesh fought
Victory is now won

Our farewell is temporary
In Thee I cast my cares
I will never forget the time and little moments
That we will always share

I wish you well in your new home
For Earth you quickly outgrew
Although many experience the walk to the land
Thee chooses only few

Rest, my sweetheart
You shall dwell in Him forever
And in due time I'll see you again
And we shall enjoy His presence together

YOU FAILED US

As I think hard on you
Sexy truth or beautiful lie
As time seems to pass
I'm too hurt to cry

I thought I knew you
The days when we were school kids
But in the test of my undeniable love
You failed my quiz

My love was wholehearted
It was swollen in abundance
From cloud nine to a market crash
It was all so sudden

My highest laughter
Is now my strongest pain
My sunny sky has turned into
Blistering rain

Why did you take me there?
The place that I hate to go
The agony of my broken heart
I can't even love anymore

The kiss of deceit I tasted
From your lips of death
Not only have you hurt my soul
But you have decreased my health

Why did you take me there?
Surely, we could have gone another way

You just had to leave me broken in pieces
No intentions to stay

So, I bid you goodbye
For I have to mend my heart
I knew that it was too good to be true
From the start

As I pick up the pieces
Of what I use to be
I smile for all the world to see
Only God sees my insides weep

I go to Him for healing
For I am His creation
I rebuke all of the evil you gave willingly
Never will I yield to that temptation

YOU FAILED US!

MY LOST LOVE

I never thought I would find him
He disappeared overnight
My love, my heartbeat
Whose eyes were black as the night

Before he left me he showed me so much passion
He had my body filled with ecstasy and rage
Our love was stronger than anything
His body left me in a daze

I never thought he would leave me
Anxious and full of delight
He had my emotions in a cup ready to drink it
In his cup of life

I wait in my room
Hoping that he comes back
Because when we reunite
My love will flow freely, and that's a fact

Do I hear a knock at the door?
Is it him God, from heaven above
It is with his romantic glow
My lost, but now found love!

HIGHWAY OF INTENTIONS

You left me for dead
On love's empty highway
Gone forever in sorrow
No intentions to stay

The two-way street of love
Has become a dead end
Sinking to rise no more
My sorrow begins

Imperfection was I
Perfection I thought you to be
You brought temporary happiness
My joy now ceased

No ambulance to rescue
The heart of the sore
The corpse of my flesh
Spills love's gore

So, at my last breath
I drive, you walk away
Departed forever in sorrow
No intentions to stay

COVERED

Sometimes I wonder
Why am I still here?
Life is so temporary
Time is drawing near

Broken into pieces
Nowhere to turn
Trying to fix myself
My soul yearns

I thought I was healing
After the pain I endured
But instead, I allowed strangers in my kingdom
Spirit subdued

I stepped away from the toxin
That was made to poison me
Didn't know I was that dirty
Too blind to see

Reacquainted with my dear friend
Someone I could always count on
We walked and talked in the garden
Indivisible bond

Though demons come to destroy me
His unchanging Hand covers me
Hiding me in plain sight
The enemy still couldn't get to me

Clothed with grace
Presence of evil all around

Covered in His mercy
Heavenly bound

Prepared with armor
Enemies in utter shock
My refuge is my defender
I stand in victory on a solid rock

WE BEEN THROUGH

It's been a month
I'm surprised you called me
How could you possibly think?
That we were meant to be

No phone calls
No quality time
No hugs and kisses
Now it's my love that you're missing

You think I'm a fool
I know your game
You thought that I would be another chick
In your hall of fame

Now you say you love me
Boy, please
You couldn't get me back
Even if you fell on your knees

I'm a grown woman
I don't have time for you
A month ago, you said "IT'S OVER"
HMPH…WE BEEN THROUGH

IN AND OUT OF TIME

I wish I could go back in time
And see your wonderful smile
Hugging and kissing me
With your own style

Holding my hand
Whispers in my ear
No darkness in sight
My midnight is clear

Making sweet love
Gentle and slow
While my love for you
Continues to grow

Take me to your land
Population: me and you
Alone at last
Our love is shining through

Kiss my lips gently
Take me to your world
Lead me to a place
Filled with white doves

Hearts flowing
Flowers blooms
Loving each other
Like lovers do

So, give me your heart
And I will give you mine
Take me in and out
In and out, in and out of time

UNFORTUNATE WHORE (PART 1)

Shake dat butt
Spread dem legs
Ride me, baby
Give me head

Bend over, slut
Take this hit
I gotta buss this nut
Right quick

You're a dumb hoe
You ain't doing it right
I got girls who would pay
To get this delight

Man, forget this
I'm about to leave
Who knew that my step-daddy
Would rape me

UNFORTUNATE WHORE (PART 2)

Sitting in a chair
My body is sore
I see my mother
Coming in my door

She wonders why I'm bleeding
Why is she so naive ?
A man so evil
She chooses to believe

She ask me was I on my cycle
No, I was raped
By your husband you love so dear
A man I can't escape

She slaps me, she says I'm lying
He's too great to do such a thing
He loves you, girl
Just as much as he loves me

He tortures my body
Day in and day out
He raped me so many times today
I lost count

So stay with him if you want to
I see that my feelings don't count
Come tomorrow morning
I'm moving out

Don't try to stop me
I'm better off in the street than here
Your daughter, who you repeatedly neglect
For a man you love so dear

TWO SPECIAL GIFTS (PART 1)

It's not sex, it's making love
When I feel his deep thrust
He got my soul on fire
Like a spontaneous combust

Kisses on my neck
Gripping of my thighs
Makes his and my
Nature rise

Two months after making love
My stomach started to shove
May be its my period, maybe it's gas
I hope whatever it is will pass

I'm rushed to the hospital
My body is weak
The doctor does many tests on me
He said I'm a few weeks into pregnancy

That not all, he had more news
Part of me burns, part of me bruised
Not only are you pregnant, but from what I see
Child, you have HIV

Oh, my God, why me
My soul, my hearts bleeds
From love that I mistakenly sought
Now I got two special gifts I didn't want

TWO SPECIAL GIFTS (PART 2)

Now I'm sitting in a corner
My mind in a pace
While the disease tears up
My body's secret place

I'm getting bigger by the second
As I hide in my room
I can't see it as a room of love
But the legion of doom

I called the boy yesterday
He say "it ain't mine"
"I got what I wanted"
"You worth less than a dime"

As he hangs up the phone
I stare in the mirror at myself
It must be my imagination
I can hear my baby crying for help

I see a knife on the counter
I still hear its plea
I decide to kill her
And me

Me and her in heaven
No regrets, no worries
Safe from anyone knowing
The real story

Suddenly I hear my alarm go off
The two gifts were just a dream
No baby, no disease
Both me and him are HIV free

SLEEPING BEAUTY

Hush little baby, don't you cry
Mama's gonna sing you a lullaby

Isn't she lovely?
I must say, she is a beautiful sight
Many people would never know
She becomes a monster at night

I want to understand her
Society only sees monsters as something bad
Never asking the questions of, who hurt them?
Who made them go mad?

I remember when she met him
She was only sixteen
He pretended like he loved her
Deep down he was just a sex fiend

She opened up the most beautiful part of her
She shared her hopes and dreams
Only for him to use and abuse her
Leaving her with scattered pictures and insecurities

Why did you wake her?
She never tried to hurt anybody
The little girl balled up inside of her
All she wanted to do is love somebody
And for somebody to love her back

She never wanted to be a killer
I guess it was the cards she was dealt
Heartbreak after heartbreak
I can only imagine how that little girl felt

She decided to turn into every man who hurt her
Sharing her flower for all to see
After all nobody cared about the little girl
So why should she

As the monster grew stronger
The little girl crawls in her own corner
Oh, how I wish I could get to her
Unconsciously join her

Listen to her every hurt
And every heartache
And every cry
Forever being the person who wipes her beautiful eyes

I would tell her this isn't who she is
You don't have to be who hurt you
Even through all the evilness
I still see that little girl inside you

As I tame the beautiful beast
I see her emerge out from the deep
I finally get to look in the mirror
The little girl is me

I'm sorry for ever abandoning you
Leaving you alone and broken
Having you waiting for me to love you
Balled up in a corner, wishing and hoping

That I would come back to you
And love you...I mean love me
You can rest better now beauty
Sleep, just sleep

BURDENED SENSATION

Good morning sunshine
You already knew it was me
I am the rain from a hurricane
That you don't like to see

I am the unbearable sensation
Entering your body from the outside in
It feels like the Almighty God
Is punishing you- for all your sin

It's electric

Baby, I am the boa
Oh, how I love to squeeze
Especially at night when you are
Trying to put your body at ease

I am that gradual shock
That starts at your fingertips
You try to meditate and pray me out
But I'm the captain of this ship

I am the boogeyman
That creature that gives your body chills
How dare you try to erase my essence
By taking your pills

You can't kick me out
The unwanted roommate, I'm staying
Oh, she just took her pills again
And oh, hell now she praying

All these affirmations and meditations
Girl, please give it up
I am the sting from your failures
I am the bitterness from life's cup

She eating right and working out
I laugh while she jogs in place
I make you tired at your inconvenience
I'll make sure you won't finish this race

Man, she a tough fighter
Old girl can take a hit
I hit her with every spasm known to man
She just won't quit

Her voice grows louder as she prays
My power grows weak
It gets harder and harder to squeeze her
Out of her mouth, life speaks

As much as I tease her
I kinda admire her resilience
She been sticking to a routine lately
How she power-walks to Rick James is brilliant

So today I loosen the squeeze
Take a little break from the prowl
I turn off the sensation for you
Just for now

TRAPPED IN MY OWN CLOSET

I got a confession
The feelings I have for you
Is quite an obsession
So strong and humbly true

My feelings in a conflict
It goes against by belief
In a battle within myself
Body filled with grief

So used to the same thing
In my life you have brought change
I knew you were special
Before I knew your name

While your class is in section
I have female erections
I'm always second guessin'
Are you a sin or a blessin'

My mom would have a fit
if she knew about you
Your walk, your talk
Your demeanor too

My family won't agree
The life that I live
Even you don't know
The love I want to give

So, I stay locked away
Wanting to explode like a rocket
Drowning in my own despair
Trapped in my own closet

COLORED

I am colored
But not under extenuating circumstances
I see myself as colored
Not as a race, but as an emotion
Through time I have evolved into a color
Depicting how I feel
Somedays I may be blue, because of depression
Others I am red,
Because you or YOU have made me angry
But still, I hide my emotion under a mask
Deep down I am afraid to let my color be seen
 So, I remain black n white
 I went to church one morning
 And I talk to my spiritual leader and he told me
 That if God is for me, who can be against me
 My color changed to a rainbow
Not what the world says it means but
What it truly is
 The token that God gave to Noah
No longer afraid to reveal my light
Like a spectrum or
How a rainbow comes in the sky after a rainy day
Oh, I have no care in the world
Or how others feel, because I know myself
So, today is a new day
Because I know who I am and what I stand for
 I am beautiful, I am intelligent, I am sad
 I am angry, I am wonderful, I am extraordinary,
And best of all...I AM COLORED!

FERTILE NINJAS

YOU THOUGHT YOU COULD DESTROY ME
TRICK YOU THOUGHT WRONG
YOU STILL WITH THAT BULLSH*T
MAN, I THOUGHT YOU WAS GROWN

WHEN WE FIRST GOT TOGETHER
IT WAS ALRIGHT
UNTIL BABY MOMMAS START POPPING UP
ALL ON MY SOCIAL SITES

YOU NEED TO CONTROL YOUR DOGS
THEY GOT ONE TIME TO COME AT ME WRONG
THAT DAMAGE I WOULD DO
WILL LEAVE THEIR HAIR DRAGGING ALONG

YOUR KISSES WERE SO SWEET
THEY MADE ME WATER
TOO BAD I WASNT THE ONLY ONE
YOU FIRST CLASS ADULTERER

SO I LET YOU GO
YOU BLAME THE BREAKUP ON ME
BUT TWO WEEKS LATER
YOU GOT A CHICK IN YOUR PHOTOS THAT AIN'T ME

YEAH YOU PLAYED DIRTY
I GOT TO ADMIT
BUT I GET THE LAST LAUGH
AS I SAY "THIS IS IT"

SO NOW I'M MOVING ON
LEARNING TO LOVE MYSELF NOW

I TREAT ME BETTER
NO BABY MOMMA CROWD

SO LIVE YOUR LIFE
AND I WILL LIVE MINE
OH I FORGOT
YOU MAKING BABIES 3-9

DAMN DUDE YOU FERTILE
I THOUGHT YOU WOULD KNOW BETTER
FROM THIS GIRL TO THAT GIRL
WE AIN'T NEVER GETTING BACK TOGETHER

I WISH YOU WELL IN LIFE
'CAUSE YOU NEED IT FOR REAL
THE WAY YOU LIVE
IS A DEAL OR NO DEAL

UNITED

Sista to Sista
Brotha to Brotha
We should all be
Lovin each other

United as one
Filled with love
Having faith
In the One Above

We've been slaves too long
Now it's time to break free
Free from worries
Free from misery

Loosen my chains
Unshackle my feet
My freedom is like a drum
Forever it beats

So join with me
Let's fellowship with hands
United
We stand!

(And divided we get played)

THE FEAST

He's ready for the feast
That lingers in her bed
He begins to lick his lips
As he separates her legs

Making more of her juices run
All over his face
Exercising his tongue
At a desiring pace

She releases her feast
All around his mouth
It's the best he ever had
And there is no doubt

Sucking her pearl
Making her scream
Now she's ready
For the peach to cream

Dig deeper with your spoon
Make her run over
He's getting seconds and thirds
There is no leftovers

So eat it all up
Make her cream
The party is over
I got one hell of a feast

EVIL SPIRIT

Surrounded by the dead
Chilling atmosphere
My heart is racing
The monster is near

Running from fear
Trying to forget the past
Praying that the horror
Won't last

I run faster and faster
This creature is quick
His smell and horrid odor
Makes my soul sick

I stumble but keep running
The air grows still
I see a bride of opportunity
The tunnel of hope gradually fills

As I see the light grown brighter
The end of my runner's high
The demon grows weaker
His power abruptly dies

Free from his world
Never to return again
This creature is not just a demon
He is my ex-boyfriend

CYBERWORLD

Click my keys
Massage my mouse
Get my monitor technologically
Aroused

I'm ready to reboot
My motherboard in a race
Ready for your
Cyberchase

So start up
My internet browser
It ain't dial-up
It takes less than an hour

So exit
The Windows Media Player
And enter into my
Windows Movie Maker

Open my file
And click everything new
So you can see my
Blank paper in view

Come fill me up
With all your letters
Its computer love
It gets no better

UNDESERVING LOVE

People don't understand
Don't even want to know why
That it's only one man
Who's always on my mind

His smell, his touch
His hug, his kiss
Makes me feel and breathe
Sheer bliss

I can't explain it
It takes more than one word
The way he says my name
Is as gentle as a bird

If we ever shall part
I wouldn't be sad
'Cause -he was the very best man
I ever had

If I were to leave this earth tomorrow
I hope he finds someone unique
Someone who will love and cherish him
More than me

CREATION (I AM)

Naked we came
Naked we shall leave
Only sin has to be
Covered with leaves

The light within
Shows through your shame
When God finally
Gives you a new name

When life is more
Than what you see
When life is greater
Than what you believe

He is within me
His Word I take
Every step, every turn
Every move I make

In His eyes
It is a celebration
I am
His creation

A GENTLEMAN'S HEART

I hate to see her sad
Broken and confused
No more hope for love
Thrown away and feeling used

I wish I could hold her
Put her mind at ease
And never let her go
In the summer's breeze

Touch her like she's never been touched
Kiss her like she's never been kissed
Making her body feel pure ecstasy
Of sweet and unadulterated bliss

Oh, I just want to love her
Until there is no more left in me
I would orbit around her world
If only she would let me

I AM..AND YOU ARE!

I AM THE TRUTH
DISTINGUISHED FROM THE BIASED YOU
I MARCH TO THE BEAT OF MY OWN DRUM
I PLAY SOLO
I AM THE CAPTAIN OF MY OWN SHIP
WHILE YOU ARE JUST A CREWMEMBER
I AM GRACEFUL AS AN EAGLE
YOU ARE THE HATRED BENEATH MY WINGS.
I AM ME
YOU ARE YOU
THERE IS NO COMPARISON.
I AM A CHILD OF GOD
AND YOU ARE TOO
BUT I WALK WITH HIM
AND YOU CHOOSE TO WALK ALONE.
FAREWELL YOU!!!

ALL I NEED

It's just one of those moments
That I don't wish to share
No need for a speech or monologue
I just want someone to care

Through my trials
And through my pain
I only ask for a glimpse of sunshine
Instead of troubling rain

In the midst of despair
I need you as a guide
When the world attacks me
In your arms I can hide

As the years grow shorter
Time seems to pass by
Through the tears I press on
As you stand by my side

Because life goes on
Pressing on in spite of the pain
All I need is Your sunshine
Instead of hurricanes

I DON'T KNOW

He says he loves me
But sometimes he fronts on me
I want this relationship to grow
But sometimes, I don't know

He wines me and dines me
But in the crowds he shuns me
I wonder where this relationship will go
But as of now, I don't know

I know he loves me
Majority of the time, he adores me
His attitude switches to and fro'
But, still I don't know

He confuses me
He enlightens me
He gives me the urge to know
But, yet I still don't know

I love him and he loves me
Adore him and he adores me
God, tell me which way to go
'Cause I'm tired of saying, "I don't know"

GREATEST SHOW ON EARTH
featuring Unconscious Mind

I got my stage set up
So you can perform tonight
You always have an excellent performance
Puts me in a delight

Kissing my notes
Nibling on my mics
The way you do me
Is a wonderful sight

Sing into my tightness
Hit dat high pitch
You got that kind of power
That got me sick
Let me tap on your keys
Bending you over the table
Your waterfall is my bass
Your moaning is my treble

As you ride my staff
Without any hesitation
You deserve an Oscar, baby
Standing ovation

So scat deep in my stomach
Make my heart race
The crowd screaming encore
On this showcase

My performance will last all night for you
I'll put in some extra hours

The action goes from the bed
To the shower

Baby feel all of my power inside you
When you ride me to the morning
Ooooo baby, you got me calling your name
The show must go on even after I came

An excellent performance like you said
We have to change the sheets
'Cause we sweat up the bed

INTO ME

I am in love y'all
And this is the first time I can say that I
Am sure about this one
I been watching this sexy thing since we were kids
It was something about them.
At first, I ain't really notice all that cuteness
Even in that teenage awkward stage, bae was still fine and turning heads
I remember at prom, baby didn't have a date
Sound kind of sad but ended up dancing with everybody else date
Such the life of the party

That Thang matured on me and things started growing and poking out
I just had to have them
But then they disappeared
And I wondered what happened to them
I heard through the grape vine that for years my sweet baby felt ugly

I saw the relationships they were in.
Stared and watched from the background and wondered why they chose all those losers
Damn I wish you would Choose me baby
When I finally saw my baby. They had some changes.
Baby was thicker than the last time we shared time and space
But I like that shit

I finally looked them in the eye and told them baby you the one I've been wanting for all my life and if you would have me
I will show you that I'm all you need in this life of sin
I knew that choosing me would take time and some level of understanding and maturing
But today I can say that they...me finally chose me. And that sexy thang is all mine to love and treat me like I am supposed to be treated

Cuz I really like What I do to me
I can't really explain it
I'm so into me

CAUGHT UP

I love him but he had to become a present memory
As much as I want him to be my everything
He already has a beautiful destiny
I'm CAUGHT up

Never would have thought that I would be the August to his winter even
though I am not the center of his joy
Every time you express your love to me, I see your right eye marry her and
the other eye make love to me. How is that possible?
I could never be jealous of her or a woman period
But I will say what makes us caught up in this entangled collision
She may be the piano to your favorite melody
But I am the soul to every song on your playlist
She may be the damsel that you can't help but save
But I am the villain in the cat suit that you always crave
She is the alpha and omega of your thoughts
But I'm always in the middle of your fantasy
Her essence got you by the hand but it's my voice that got you by the lips dammit
I'm up and I'm stuck on him
And as much as I want to try to hate him so that I can move on
I hear his voice in my ear whenever I kiss another man
I feel his bottom lip on my neck when I'm washing dishes
I have visions of him giving me something I can feel when I'm trying to sleep
2 seconds from missing deadlines at work because I want him to feast on me
Shit... just leave me be
No please stay
I said muthafucka just leave
No don't end it this way
At least kiss me goodbye before you go
And when you leave try not to say my name in the middle of your I DO

VOCAL RAIN

I can't wait for him to get home.
I don't know what it is but when he's had a long day at work, he takes all of his frustration out on me
It excites me!
Sometimes I pick an argument just so he can make passionate love to me
Hey daddy I been waiting for you...how was work
Another long day. Poor baby. But I have something that'll make you feel much better
Go take a shower first and I'll make your plates.
I cooked a nice dinner, but that's not the only plate I want you to lick clean.
Soon as he walks out of the shower, I have his first plate ready, face down ass up
He said damn baby you so selfish and proceeded to walk over to the head of the bed. Let daddy feed you first
He loves the way his microphone rubs against my vocals and make me hit high notes without touching me-yet
He grabs my hair and then kisses my lips whispering that he wanted me to be his good little Byrd.
As much as he loves me, he loves Byrd the most
He turns me over slowly giving me his manhood. He loves looking into my brown eyes with his hand around my neck. Moving his hips like he is stirring coffee hitting my spot while my walls hug him.
The "oh shit" and the "oh fuck" almost got the best of him so he started eating his 1st plate. He sucks on my clit and lips with his tongue and lips making me wetter as he grips my thighs so I can't run. And when we lock eyes, I can't help but sing to him even more

NOVELIST

There was a time when
I was an open book
Full of words that captured you as soon as you read the first page
Best seller
I was never afraid to share my vivid and candid masterpiece to the world
Until people started turning their nose up at the words on my pages
I find it funny that people I loved and admired started treating my novel
like they do the Bible
Crossing out things that are too uncomfortable to read
Underlining stuff I've said and paraphrasing it to justify how to treat me
Bookmarking days of journal entry that they found hilariously chaotic and
Highlighting all of my mistakes
It was the question mark mixed with dried tear drops on my 24th
summer that did it for me
I took my book off the shelves. Never to be read by the public again
Of course I wrote a little here and little there over time but I refused to
share it until I met a series of authors that wanted to collab with me.
Well, they are history now but they had me telling everything about
my novel and had me changing my climax just so it could fit into their
plot creating peculiar outcomes. Some of my pages were ripped and
burned to shreds, only leaving one page left.
And as much as I have the urge to start over, I leave that page empty
never to tarnish its innocence

WELCOME HOME, ME

Hey...it's just me
Kenni and Byrd are asleep so it's just me
I don't speak as much because no one wants to hear me so I hide myself
Been doing it for so long that it becomes natural

It started when that older boy in the neighborhood kissed me.
I was only 5
I saw my oldest sister get touched by my cousin

I got kicked out of middle school because my because my boyfriend, who was too damn old me, threatened to do harm to a girl at school, but since I was a good student the principal withdrew me and I went to another school to finish off 8th grade

In high school I was talking to a guy online and we were talking spicy and the screen froze. Not knowing I left to go to the restroom and by the time I came back, the class made up a nickname for me and I wasn't even sexually active at that time. Hello Anxiety

I was 16 when I gave away my flower to my boyfriend and that's all because he gave me an ultimatum that if I didn't he would break up with me so I did and he still left

I gave my heart to a guy at 17 and he cheated on me with a girl from my school and he hit me so Kenni took over for 6 years and Byrd made appearances on days we had to go to church. I was hid

Kenni fell for a dude that was on drugs so Byrd took over. Byrd fell in love with Mr and he tried to destroy her so I cried for all of us. She sang, I cried, and Kenni acted out off and on sexually for 3 years.

I finally stopped crying and met someone. I really liked him, Kenni was on the fence about it, and Byrd didn't want no parts of it either. I fell in love and for 2 years I found myself being mistreated all over again. Hello depression, welcome back anxiety, and oh shit hey panic attacks. And the sisters did what they also do, take over!

I been missing myself lately
The last time I looked in a mirror I was sucked into a broken vessel that didn't deserve the healing power I possessed

It's amazing the pieces I broke off myself just so the leech could thrive
He left only enough for me to bare the most precious seed inside of me

The seed was the gift from the Almighty that molded me into the Mother of past present and future tense
It allowed us...me to evolve unto something more beautiful Than before

Although parts of me are still broken
The cracks in me is proof that I'm still alive
She was persecuted but never left alone
Cast down but not destroyed
I don't look like what I been through because my soul is restored

Welcome home...Me

OH NOAH

Noah Noah
Where for ark thou, Noah
Don't deny thy water or refuse thy rain
It's is with great urgency that you say my name
As I howl at the moon
Like the wolves that joined us in travel
Be the lion to my jungle
Make me unravel
Trunk long and gargantuan like African elephants
Made my love come down and then you heaven sent
Me into another dimension
Oh what a succulent, melanated vision
Juices pouring as abundant as Atlantic
While he journeyed my voyage to Atlantis
And I always come back for him
It was
40 days and 40 nights of a whirlwind
By day 38 I almost through a towel in
Until the bird in me flew and reached sun moon mountains and rivers
Each gush of waters made my wings shiver
Finally bringing him the branch of honor
He made it to my land of abundance and no longer will he thirst for
another water
And I can't wait for him to weather my flood again

ALTERED SENSE

It's something about watching you
You don't even have to do anything and I just want to look at you
I ain't no stalker but every time I get a glimpsed of your shadow I wanna
capture it in my peripheral and make love to you sideways
It's the purple haze and grateful dead that has me giving you wonder
with my head and my name ain't even Stevie
I just want you to be the sativa to my ecstasy giving me long back shots
of your Hennessey
Cum baby and devour me
I'm that pool of liquor drown for me
Touch my walls and pound for me
Making me squirt clitorally
Let me be your Mary Jane while you slurp my chocolate baileys
Giving you a sugar rush inhaling this pink kush
It's exotic as I move my hypnotic with each stroke on your ganga
So baby let's get faded on our own supply
You give me that natural high

Baby I want you...na na
Why can't I keep my fingers off you baby
I want you na na

FLY BAG LADY

He loves me
But I don't think he is supposed to
You see I got suitcases of sins, mental instability, and heartache that even I have a tough time carrying

Generational curses mixed with present hexes and a side of futuristic tribulations prevents me from showing him I adore him
I am a walking train wreck

It's amazing how he sees the beauty in the midst of my catastrophe.
Where did you get those kinds of eyes?
Or does everyone have them
If so then people have options of if they want to love or destroy

So will you adore me or treat me like another street whore ?
What are your intentions with me?
Tell me now because I can't afford another burden...I mean bag to carry

This smart ass

Told me that as much as he craved me like that sweet potato pie his grandma used to make on Sunday; He wanted to see me grow, receive love, and be balanced because he loved me different
He even told me that even though my wings are clipped I can still fly
But I had to get rid of the bags that's weighing me down

As much as it scares me, I trust him enough to believe everything he has said. To heal not for the sake of him but for the sake of all of me

Depression bag baby
Let it go (4x)
Anxiety bag yeah

Bet your love can make it better
Panic attack bag oh yeah
Let it go (4x)
Guilt and shame bags baby
Bet your love can make it better
Insecurity bag yeah
Let it go (4x)
Low self-esteem bag baby
Bet your love can make it better
I'm flying!

WHY I DRIP?!

Hey pen, we need to talk
You've been awfully cold with me lately
You know how much I adore you and
How your words drive me crazy

Come write for me
I am in love with you, pen
The way your words touch my walls
Makes me feel invincible to every sin

I am addicted to how you write my name
And rub your lyrics against my thighs
You make it your business to look me in my eyes
Snatching my soul

You give me sensual anxiety every time
You push it inside of me
Kisses on my neck mixed with sexual growls and screams
I break out in ballads as You make her cream

Come write for me
My page is yearning for your words
The licking and sucking on my honey
Has songs coming out of this Byrd

Don't make me over
Now that I'd do anything for you
I just want you to be the bee to my honey
Being the reason why I drip eternally

Touch me with your mouth
Making my bass treble inside

As you take your evening's dip
Your symphony makes me cum alive

Dammit pen
You make my mental hit vibratos
As you dip Your chocolate dipper
Into my moonlight sonata

Come write for me
Be the funk in my left wall and the RnB in my right
Having me drip repeatedly
With every thrust of your pipe

Come write for me
Come write in me
As your chocolate dips
Being the very reason why I drip

PURPLE IS MY COLOR

I always liked the color purple
It's my favorite color
Not just the color itself
But I liked the movie too

You know how Suge was sweet like honey
Celie was like a bee
Reminds me of rolling around in the grass
Being completely free

I remember always picking that color
In all my drawings, little girls had on a purple dress
Purple bow or a purple shoe
Better yet a purple shirt

I know people would think I'm crazy
It's just a color
But not to me
It's so much purple has done for me

Even when my spirit felt poor
It was purple that made me feel rich
I mean not just rich but wealthy
Even when I only had enough for a bag of chips

As a grew older, purple was my hope
When life beat me down with redness of rage
Or blue of depression
Purple was my phoenix after the dust settled

I tell you that color is something special
I feel like royalty even when my hair is undone

Especially when I wear a stylish purple headband
That feels better than any crown

I just want to tell purple thank you
Not just for giving me a favorite color
But giving this little girl an imagination
And the appreciation of purple reign

COCOA UNITE

Someone once said that black is something we don't get to choose but it's something we get to cherish
My sister I see you
With that cocoa brown skin and that kinky curly hair I just want to talk to you and see if our kin folks crossed paths like we did
Chocolate drop I just wanna hug you and share stories of past and present
Brown sugar we are the future
My brother come here, shake my hand
We just strangers in this land even though we been building since we were in the Middle East
Sadly it's never been justice but just us
And I just want to protect us because I love you
I need you
I value you
I uplift
I adore
I just want to restore you
And give us strength to keep being young gifted and black
Oh what a time it is to be a hue that everyone envies
Let them stay mad my magical ones
As we keep being melanated, powerful, and most importantly magical
Cocoa Unite

YOU LOVE ME DIFFERENT

Before there was a sun or moon
And as the stars graced the sky
You loved the very twinkle in my eye
I am in awe in how much you value my soul
You even put the purest part of you on the line
Just for me to always have access to you
I been caught up in so many situations but somehow the light at the
end of the tunnel never fails to appear
Thanks to you
I apologize for being ungrateful or hard headed at times but
It blows my mind that you have a Name like no other Name
Thoughts like no one else's thoughts
And you move like no one else's moves
I don't know what the future holds
But You live in me and You hold my future
In your Unchanging Hands
The same hands that made every color that I see and every sound I hear
The thunder in his voice vibrates my atmosphere while he hugs me
with his wind and showers me with his rain
Oh God how I love you
You promised me that I would want for nothing
When I'm weary you let me rest in your field and restore me
You lead me down a path that you have already covered
Even when I walk through places that I don't feel comfortable in
I'm not scared but You make your presence known
You exhibit your omnipresence around me like the moon orbits the Earth
You make a table full of things for me to enjoy while my enemies watch me
You sanctify me with your oil running my cup over
Surrounding me with your compassion and generosity every day of my life
You love me especially...different

WET NICKLES AND APPLES

If you see me walking down the street
And I start to cry each time we meet
Walk on by, walk on by

It was a smell
A very smelly smell
That was smelly.

The aroma was oh so heavy because it met my nose before I saw him
It put a twitch in my eye as soon as he walked on by
Got damn what luck
Because that's a type of aroma that makes me silently screams what the fuck
But I played it cool, poker face
With a smell like that I was two seconds from catching a case
He turned around and asked did I care for a sample
I said oh no, baby you smell like wet nickels and apples

DEAR POETRY

Dear poetry,

The hell is wrong with you?
I didn't ask you to disrupt my train of thought with words and phrases that somehow turn into stanzas
I was minding my own business until you decided to summon kindred poetic spirits to awaken my pen.
Do you even know the reason why I stopped fucking with pen?
You don't?
I'll tell you how it went.
Picture it!
A young, melanin flavored goddess meets a guy and she falls for him. He tells her he loves her while he strategically breaks her down with his Narcissism. She had a father but no father figure to teach her that boys ain't worth a damn at that age.
In the midst of tears and admiration, her pen began to write of what she thought love was with this young boy. Not only did he pluck her flower but abandoned her in a garden of despair.
He never cared
Ladies and gentleman, that young girl was me
And for years pen would find its way to make a fool of me when it came to life.
Pen had me writing stories of injustice, sexuality, love, discovery and alike
Sadly no one wanted to hear the words on the pages unless it was with a melody
I literally broke pen in half by the time I was in my twenties and told that bastard to never step foot on my doorstep again.
Never would have thought as much as I loved pen that it would hurt me like it did
When one of its friends led me back to the poetic den I thought things changed
People listened to me...for the first time people listened to me
But that soon was overshadowed by the Byrd and rebel in me that somehow became the requirement for me to be heard or I was ignored
Pen once again you pushed me into situations where people didn't really

love me but only loved the magic that was created in my
partnership with you
I don't get it?
What did I ever do to you or people for that matter to be treated like I
am worthless
Is it so much to ask to be loved without your creativity being reduced
to half dead flowers and "thank you for sharing"
News flash, Kenya they still don't want to hear you they want your pen
Dear pen, what gives?
How dare you pour my words on pages and then allow me to be treated
like a sheep being slaughtered
If you weren't going to help heal my heart this time pen then why bother
You always find a way to disturb my peace but this time I have the last say so
You made a fool of me
And honestly, I don't have the fight left in me to want to know why
So today I yield my mic and you pen
Or do I really?
Even though you and I have a toxic dynamic
I'm still stupid enough to keep partnering with you because you bring
out the artist in me
And this time I'll try not to go into a depression because you don't love
me like I love you

www.ingramcontent.com/pod-product-compliance
Lightning Source LLC
Chambersburg PA
CBHW061333120726
48001CB00002B/846